THiNK AGAiN

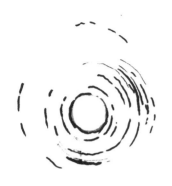

THiNK AGAiN

WRITTEN BY **JonArno Lawson**   ILLUSTRATED BY **Julie Morstad**

KCP POETRY

An Imprint of Kids Can Press

For my true love, Amy, and the little loves who sprang
from us: Sophie, Ashey and Joseph — J.A.B.L.

For Jake — J.M.

Table of Contents

Hugo

Hugo's lying in the sand

A bit of starlight in his hand

His fingers open, out it pours,

The ocean sighs, the ocean roars.

My Mind

My mind's awash in misconceptions,
ditherings, and failed connections

But now and then a new thought blooms,
straight out of all that greenery —

The mind's no mere machinery —

It's more than it itself presumes.

Thoughtless

I try to leave all thoughts behind me,
but they always know.

They start to search and start to find
me everywhere I go.

Is being thoughtless such a crime?

My thoughts seem to think so.

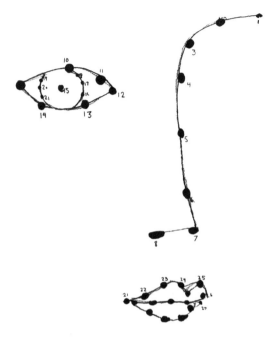

Recall

I'm trying to recall your face,

I haven't managed yet.

Why are half-remembered things

The hardest to forget?

Sit Still

Sit still said her father —

Quiet said her mom:

So she sat still and quiet

As an unexploded bomb.

Now Up, Now Down

Now up now down now down now up

The waves will toss you so

You hardly get yourself upright

When overboard you go.

What I Want

I've objected and complained

But it hasn't done any good —

I don't want to be explained

I want to be understood.

My Dad

My Dad had a mid-life crisis,
quit his wife and job.

The briefest summing up suffices:

Gave himself up to his vices

Lives on beer and pizza slices.

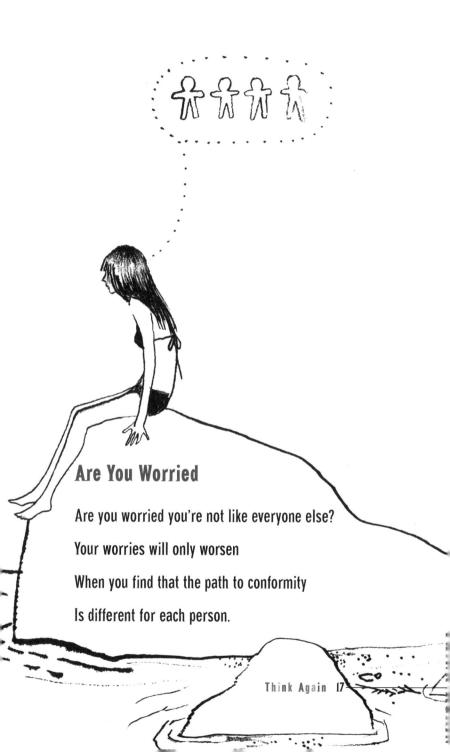

Are You Worried

Are you worried you're not like everyone else?

Your worries will only worsen

When you find that the path to conformity

Is different for each person.

Be Grateful

Be grateful for what you've got —

But if what you've got doesn't seem like a lot

You can always find comfort in the
opposite thought

And be grateful for what you haven't got.

The Three MEs

The first me is the me you know

The second you'll meet rarely.

The third me — uh oh, there he goes

Him you'll never see.

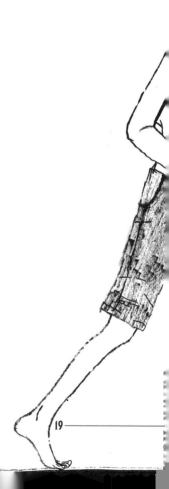

Up to Your Neck

I know that you might not agree

But it won't matter much if you're dead:

Better three days up to your neck

Than five minutes over your head.

What I Saw

I saw that you grasped it

And knew why you hesitated:

The truth may be simple

But its impact is complicated.

Think Again

Eventually a thought will come

But no one can say when:

If you think thinking's easy,

Think again.

Frame, Mask and Mirror

I'm trying to see you

You won't let me nearer

Than frame to a picture

Or mask to a mirror.

The Idea

First it struck her, then it hit her

Forcing her to reconsider — but —

Finding parts she didn't like

She changed it so it better fit her.

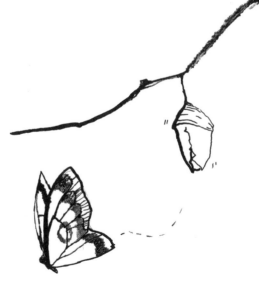

He Laughed

He laughed, but was it laughter

That you were really after

When you told him of your anger,

And warned him of the danger?

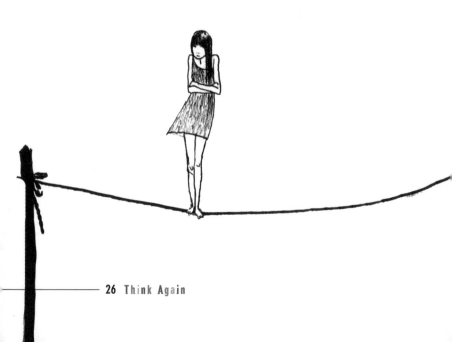

A Thought Thought Out

Frustrating, the thought thought out

From certainty back into doubt

But better this than certainties

That no one ever thinks about.

Unfulfilled Desire

How strange the ways and flinty strength

Of unfulfilled desire

That sparks and sparks through someone's life

Without once catching fire.

Time

The past cannot be paid for

And the future can't be bought:

You've got the present moment and

That's really all you've got.

Up for Grabs

i.

I'm up for grabs

Grab me if you dare —

You'll have to try to catch me unaware,

Or else you'll end up grabbing at the air.

ii.

I'm up for grabs

Grab me if you can —

The last who tried to ran and ran and ran

And ended up right back where he began.

iii.

I'm up for grabs

Grab if you desire

To have the truth inside you like a fire

Too hot to be extinguished by a liar.

iv.

I'm up for grabs

But you would never grab

You hold me knowing that I can't be held,

And knowing that to hold is not to have.

I Don't Feel Free

I don't feel free,

And things are such I want to see,
but not to touch. To be

But not to be

Too much.

My Needs

I need a little time to squander

A book to read

A place to wander

And puzzling quandaries I can ponder.

The Fever

I loved the burning fever

That filled my mind with smoke,

And missed those clouded dreams

When my fever finally broke.

Losing Track of Myself

When I saw you, I saw myself —

My self I still didn't know.

That's why, mistaking your hand for my own,

I let it go.

My Point of View

Why is it that you always

Seem to share my point of view?

I'd love just once to hear you say

"I don't agree with you."

On the Ball and Off

He's often off

And often on

And off and on

He's neither.

You're Clever

You're clever? Good. Resist the urge
To show it.
You're here not to outsmart the world
But to know it.

Out of Your Mind

Almost everyone out there's been through it:

It's as hard to get some things out of your mind

As it is to get others into it.

The Missing Conversation

The crack: almost invisible, but what seems
whole is broken —

Important words went missing

Between two

Who should have spoken.

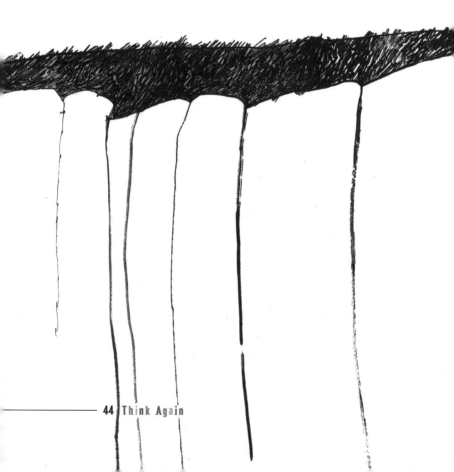

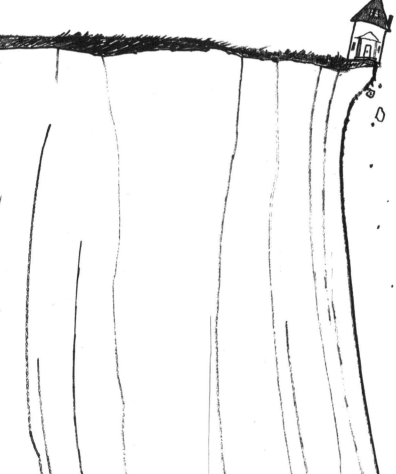

Convincing

You really want

To convince?

Stop arguing;

Use hints.

Wide Awake

Wide awake and worried, and wondering what to do:

Do I don't I will I won't I wonder so, and so

Would you if you were me I wonder though

If I would worry just as much, if I were you.

Dried Out Water

There's dried out water in my shoes

My head is bouldered in by blues

I feel unable to amuse

The worn out MEs, the used up YOUs.

Pleasant

It's pleasant to read in a darkening room

Where no one at all can intrude:

A cookie and tea and a cat on my knee

While shedding a poisonous mood.

Differences

You say:

"I accept our differences"
and offer me your hand,

But it's what we have in common

That I can't stand.

You Made Your Hurt Small

You made your hurt small

Constricted and compact;

Not easy to see,

Or once seen, to look at.

Eggs

Don't put all your eggs

in one basket!

But what if there's only one basket?
Good question!

(I'd hoped no one would ask it ...)

Time

Time comes quick and raw, it can't be

Slowed or refined

It moves so fast because

it's leaving everything behind.

Patience

I remembered, watching as you

Struggled with frustration,

That patience can't be learned

Without aggravation.

Be Careful Who You Make Friends With

Enemies

Who weren't once friends

Are often better

At making amends.

The Heart

Make sure that your heart

Isn't too well defended:

Your heart is designed

To be broken and mended.

Travelling Trees

Trees go wandering seed by seed:

In time their journey's revealed.

While you and I follow a path through
the woods,

The trees make a row through a field.

We'll Be There in a Minute

The Past? We'll be there

In a minute.

The Future? Look again —

Nobody's in it.

Oh Star I Never Wished Upon

You used to be there all the time,
beckoning and shining

And every night I turned my back,
and stared into the empty black:

I need you now — where have you gone

Oh star I never wished upon?

An Attempt at Description

How to describe the natural world?

I think I know how to begin:

A tiger has terrible, beautiful eyes,

And the night has lovely skin.

Acknowledgments

Thank you to my editor, Sheila Barry, without whom this book
would never have come to be; to Karen Li, for pointing out
the love story; and to Marie Bartholomew for the grace and beauty
of the book's design. Thanks to the OAC (via Kids Can Press) for a
Writers' Reserve Grant.

"Pizza slices," as a rhyme, was suggested by Jennifer McFadden.
Melville Orenstein came up with the line "I am the star that no one
wished upon." "Now up, now down" is the reworking of an image I
found in Hallaj (page 181 of *The Sufi Mystery*, published by The
Octagon Press, 1980). "Losing Track of Myself" was suggested by
a comment my daughter Sophie made, and "Dried Out Water" by a
comment made by my son, Ashey. David Pendlebury's masterful
translation of *The Ocean in a Jar* by Baba Tahir Hamadani
(Katchaloo, 2006) inspired and encouraged me to stick with the
quatrain form.

It seems only fair to point out that the poem "My Dad" is not at all
autobiographical.

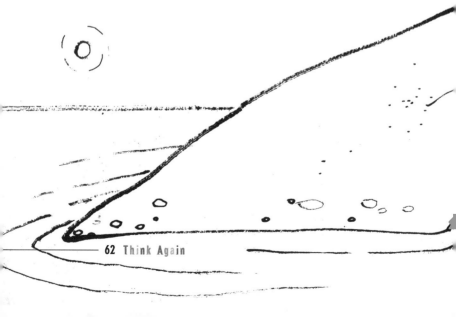

KCP Poetry is an imprint of Kids Can Press

Text © 2010 JonArno Lawson
Illustrations © 2010 Julie Morstad

"Thoughtless" and "Are You Worried" both appeared in *Black Stars in a White Night Sky* (Pedlar Press, 2006) and are reprinted here with permission.

Kids Can Press acknowledges the financial support of the Government of Ontario, through the Ontario Media Development Corporation's Ontario Book Initiative; the Ontario Arts Council; the Canada Council for the Arts; and the Government of Canada, through the BPIDP, for our publishing activity.

Published in Canada by
Kids Can Press Ltd.
29 Birch Avenue
Toronto, ON M4V IE2

Published in the U.S. by
Kids Can Press Ltd.
2250 Military Road
Tonawanda, NY 14150

www.kidscanpress.com

The artwork in this book was rendered in pen and ink.
The text is set in New Global.

Edited by Sheila Barry
Designed by Marie Bartholomew
Printed and bound in China

This book is smyth sewn casebound.

CM 10 0 9 8 7 6 5 4 3 2 1

Library and Archives Canada Cataloguing in Publication

Lawson, JonArno
    Think again / written by JonArno Lawson ; illustrated by Julie Morstad.

Poems.
ISBN 978-1-55453-423-4 (bound)

I. Children's poetry, Canadian (English). I. Morstad, Julie II. Title.

PS8573.A93T43 2010   jC811'.54   C2009-903624-X

Kids Can Press is a *CORUS*™ Entertainment company